T0008030

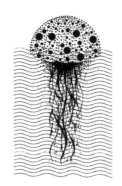

Front cover illustration by Guilherme Karsten, Brazil
The Sea Change project was initiated by The International Centre for the Picture Book in Society at the University of Worcester

First published in Great Britain and in the USA in 2023 by Otter-Barry Books,
Little Orchard, Burley Gate, Herefordshire, HR1 3QS
www.otterbarrybooks.com

ISBN 978-1-91307-418-0
Printed in Dubai

1 3 5 7 9 8 6 4 2

SEA CHANGE

Save the Ocean

Curated and edited by Tobias Hickey
of The International Centre for the Picture Book in Society

Otter-Barry BOOKS

CONTENTS

TAKE ACTION FOR THE OCEAN

My favourite fellow-creature is Prochlorococcus. It lives in the ocean and is the planet's smallest photosynthetic organism. It alone is responsible for production of 20% of the biosphere's oxygen; so, I suggest to you that we should all understand what is required to maintain the well-being of Prochlorococcus.

Ocean literacy should be on the curriculum of every school on the planet. There can be no healthy planet without a healthy ocean and, be it through over-fishing, pollution, or the effects of anthropogenic greenhouse gas emissions, the ocean's health is currently in decline. The first principle of ocean literacy is that there is one big ocean with many features, so it is logical that we do not use the possessive and plural term "our oceans". We belong to the ocean, not the other way around. In fact, in all probability the ocean will still exist long after homo sapiens has ceased to, thus it is rather deluding to claim the ocean as ours.

Following the logic of one ocean: take a look at a world map and erase all the man-made names from it. The physical reality of one big ocean becomes clear, a reality that is vital to understanding currents, pollution, ecosystems and the fact that a melting ice sheet in Greenland has direct consequences for Pacific atoll dwellers faced with the trauma of rising sea levels.

The United Nations Secretary General has pronounced a red alert for humanity. He says we have been engaged in a war against Nature and that we must make peace without further delay. Making peace with Nature means living in a world in which human hope and progress exist within a cocoon of utmost respect for Nature's requirements.

As a loving grandfather, I assert the fundamental truth that we must strive with steadfast hope towards the bright prospects for a better world that lie ahead. Taking an almost romantic inspiration from Nature, that truth is anchored in reason, not the fantasy of superheroes or the politics of denial. It is anchored in the knowledge that humanity has ample reserves of genius capable of discovering the required solutions. And as the way ahead becomes clearer, we should be confident that leaders will emerge in politics and commerce with the courage to reallocate the world's resources in the direction of sustainability, equity, and intergenerational justice.

Sabine Waldmann-Brun – Germany

For all for life: the ocean

CELEBRATING THE OCEAN

Let the sea set you free.

LET THE SEA SET YOU FREE

YUVAL ZOMMER

Yuval Zommer – UK

"The sea is like music.
It has all the dreams
of the soul
within itself and
sounds them over."

/Carl Gustav Jung/

Save Our Sea!

Andreja Peklar

ANDREJA PEKLAR

SLOVENIJA

SLOVENIJA

PREDNOSTNO
Priority

SEA CHANGE
PO BOX 17832
BIRMINGHAM
B13 3QB
U.K.

The sea is like music. It has all the dreams of the soul within itself and sounds them over.

Carl Gustav Jung

15

Meanwhile the fish
From which we all descend
Witnessed with curiosity
The collective tragedy
Of this world
Which they undoubtedly
must have deemed evil
And they began to think
In their great sea...

From How Deep the Sea Is
by Lucio Dalla

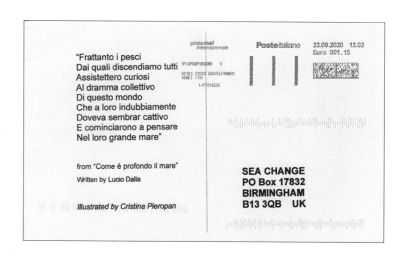

"Frattanto i pesci
Dai quali discendiamo tutti
Assistettero curiosi
Al dramma collettivo
Di questo mondo
Che a loro indubbiamente
Doveva sembrar cattivo
E cominciarono a pensare
Nel loro grande mare"

from "Come è profondo il mare"
Written by Lucio Dalla

Illustrated by Cristina Pieropan

SEA CHANGE
PO Box 17832
BIRMINGHAM
B13 3QB   UK

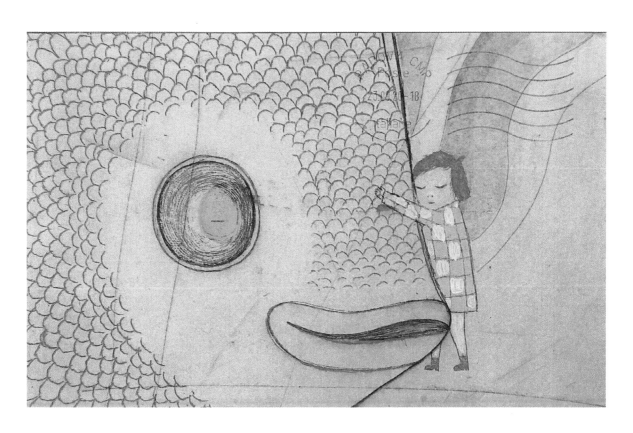

17 Cristina Pieropan – Italy

I'd like to be under the sea
in an octopus's garden
in the shade.

Ringo Starr

Hedie Meischke – The Netherlands

Jane Ray – UK

Little Fish

The tiny fish enjoy themselves
In the sea.
Quick little splinters of life,
Their little lives are fun to them
In the sea.

D.H. Lawrence 1885-1930

SAVE OUR OCEANS!
SAVE OUR WHALES!
and mermaids too...

i Love you BLue!

Save our oceans!
Save our whales!
and mermaids too...

I love you Blue!

23

Barroux – France

When she was a small child I painted her, sleeping. The counterpane was an ocean where dolphin, whales, small boats with sails, sand dollars and starfish patterned in plenty.

Now she is grown and she follows the sea road, the whale road, while shooting stars thread their lights across the sky.

And she sends me pictures of the children of whales, such signs of hope.

Sperm Whale's Child

25

Jackie Morris – UK

Among the corals
Deep down you swim
Skin so thick
With scales so thin
In clean water
Is where you gleam
No plastic waste
Completely free

Amongst the corals
Deep down you swim
Skin so thick
With scales so thin
In clean water
Is where you gleam
No plastic waste
Completely free

- Sena Ahadji -

SEA CHANGE
PO BOX 17832
BIRMINGHAM
B13 3QB
UK

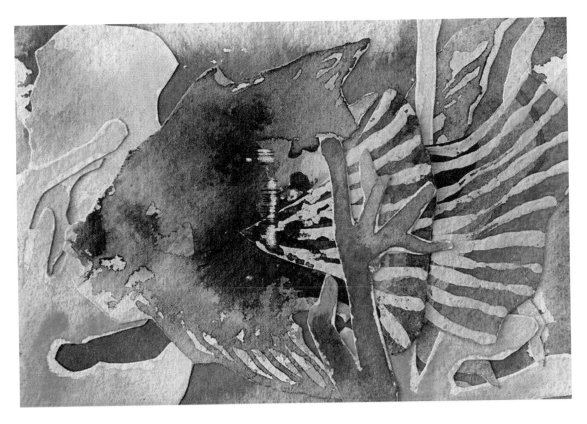

27   Sena Ahadji – Ghana

Dear Tobias

Here's my entry for
SEA CHANGE ~
JENGU, the mermaid.

Regards

Ken

© Ken Wilson-Max 2020

Royal Mail Mount Pleasant
01-09-2020 Mail Centre

SEA CHANGE
P.O. BOX 17832
Birmingham
B13 3QB
UK

ken@kenwilsonmax.com

Jengu, The Mermaid

The Sawa people of Cameroon
worship the Jengu. She is said
to have long hair and a
beautiful smile.

Jengu, The Mermaid

The Sawa people of Cameroon worship the Jengu. She is said to have long hair and a beautiful smile.

Ken Wilson-Max – UK/Zimbabwe

"To look at the sea
is to become what
one is"
    Eteh Adnan

These words by Eteh
Adnan (poet and
artist) reflect how
I feel about the sea,
the world and me.
My artwork is lino
print.
    Maja Stanic
www.majaglassstudio.co.uk

SEA CHANGE
PO BOX 17832
BIRMINGHAM
B13 3QB

To look at the sea is to become what one is.

Eteh Adnan

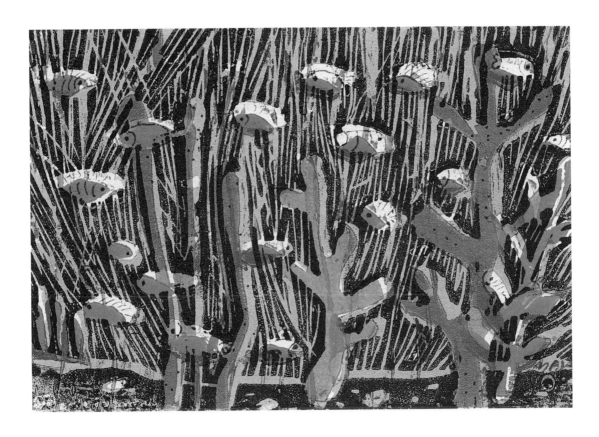

31   Maya Stanic, UK/Bosnia and Herzegovina

The home we seek is in eternity. The truth we seek
is like a shoreless sea of which your paradise is but a drop.

The Conference of the Birds – *Attar of Nishapur*

33   Mohammad Barrangi Fashtami– UK/Iran

Piet Grobler – South Africa   34

"There are 5 oceans and 113 seas on earth," said big fish
"We can keep swimming for a long, long time" said the little one

I. SEA CHANGE
PO BOX 17832
BIRMINGHAM
B13 3QB
U.K.

piet probler

"There are 5 oceans and 113 seas on Earth," said big fish. "We can keep swimming for a long, long time," said the little one.

SEA
THE BEAUTY
OF THE
SEA

Nelleke Verhoeff – Netherlands   36

Sea
The beauty
of the sea.

The ocean is our home.

39

Martí Alcon – Spain

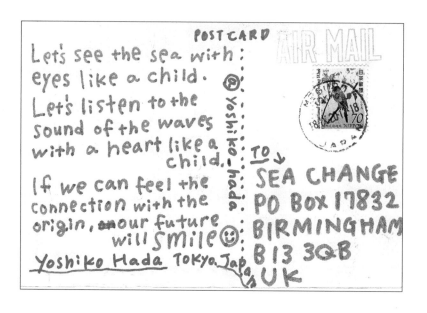

Let's see the sea with eyes like a child.
Let's listen to the waves with a heart like a child.
If we can feel the connection with the origin,
our future will smile.

41

Yoshiko Hada – Japan

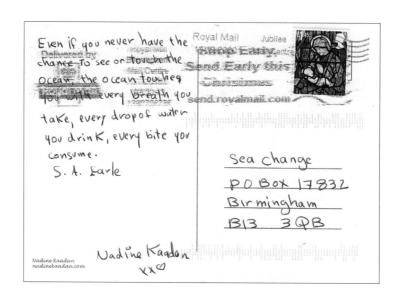

Even if you never have the chance to see or touch the ocean, the ocean touches you with every breath you take, every drop of water you drink, every bite you consume.

S.A. Earle

43   Nadine Kaadan – UK/Syria

Love Sea
Save Sea

45

Mimi Azrin – Malaysia

Axel Scheffler – UK/Germany

Save our Seas! Says **O**ld (Axel) **S**cheffler

DANGER TO THE OCEAN

"It's surely our responsibility to do everything within our power to create a planet that provides a home not just for us, but for all life on Earth."
— Sir David Attenborough

Artist — Kathleen Richens

SEA CHANGE
PO BOX 17832
BIRMINGHAM
B13 3QB
UK

"It's surely our responsibility to do everything within our power to create a planet that provides a home not just for us, but for all life on Earth."

Sir David Attenborough

49   Kathleen Richens – New Zealand

seaseaseaseaseaseaseaseaseasea

RB.

2020

51 Renata Bueno – Brazil/Portugal

Marion Deuchars – UK

52

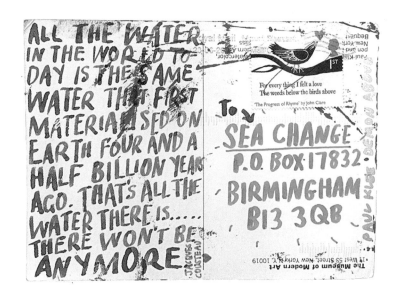

All the water in the world today is the same water that
first materialised on Earth four and a half billion years ago.
That's all the water there is....
There won't be any more.

POST CARD

1·3·21

PMC CFCP 457

08. 03. 21 06h40

SCHOOLS CLOSE

WHEN ENROLLMENT

NUMBERS COLLAPSE.

Julie McAllister

PERTH WESTERN AUSTRALIA

SARDINE : FISH SUSTAINABLY.

Support
Australia

To: SEA CHANGE

PO BOX 17832

BIRMINGHAM

B133QB U.K.

AUSTRALIA $3.50
Riverland wetland, SA

Schools close
when enrollment
numbers collapse.

55 Julie McAllister – Australia

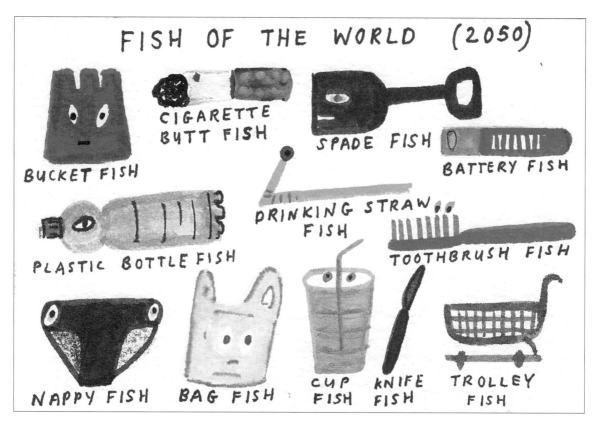

Sarah Millin – UK

There will be more plastic than fish
in the ocean by 2050.

Ellen MacArthur Foundation

LET'S BAN PLASTIC (single use) NOW.

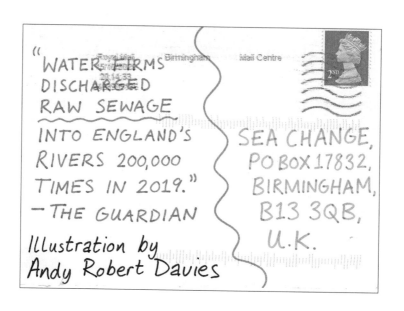

"WATER FIRMS DISCHARGED RAW SEWAGE INTO ENGLAND'S RIVERS 200,000 TIMES IN 2019."
— THE GUARDIAN

Illustration by Andy Robert Davies

SEA CHANGE,
PO BOX 17832,
BIRMINGHAM,
B13 3QB,
U.K.

"Water firms discharged raw sewage into England's rivers 200,000 times in 2019."

The Guardian

59   Andy Robert Davies – UK

Karol Bernal – Spain

60

SEA CHANGE POSTCARD
CREATE FOR the SEA
CHANGE Exhibition IN AiD
of an environmental
charity.

" Si EL MAR
MUERE
EL MUNDO
MUERE "

Rte: Karol bernal
karolbernal@gmail
.com

SEA CHANGE
P.O. BOX 17832
BIRMINGHAM
B13 3QB
UNITED KINGDOM

If the sea dies
the world dies

Forget the White Sea.
Forget the Black Sea,
Forget the Red Sea.
What we will have,
Is the one and only the Dead Sea.

Jaan Kaplinski – Estonian poet

63

Viive Noor – Estonia

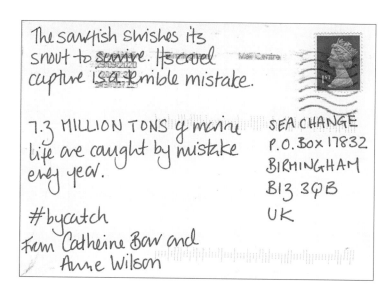

The sawfish swishes its snout to survive.
Its cruel capture is a terrible mistake.

7.3 million tons of marine life are caught
by mistake every year. #bycatch

64

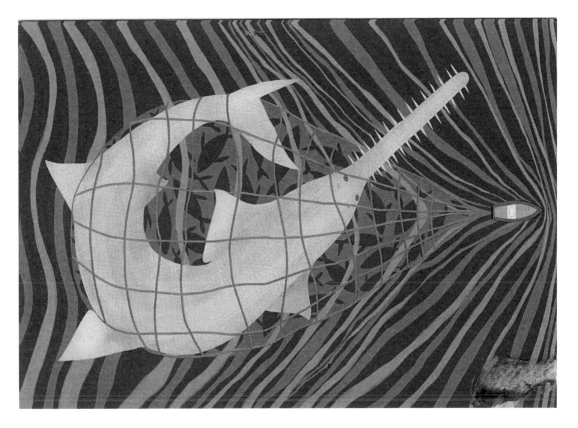

65   Catherine Barr and Anne Wilson – UK

Should you see God in the
Heartbeats of the Garden,
Hasten to say:
The fish pond is without water.
The wind was visiting the
Plane tree.
I was on my way to God!

The Fishes Convey a Message – *Sohrab SePehri*

67 Ali Ghorbanimoghaddam – Germany/Iran

Varvara Iashchenko – Norway/Russia   68

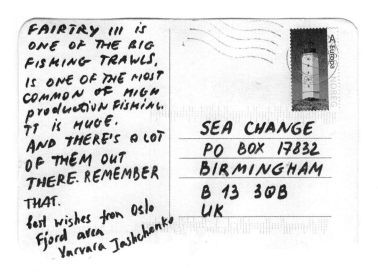

FAIRTRY III is ONE OF THE BIG FISHING TRAWLS, IS ONE OF THE MOST COMMON OF HIGH production fishing. IT IS HUGE. AND THERE'S a LOT OF THEM OUT THERE. REMEMBER THAT.
Best wishes from Oslo Fjord area
Varvara Jashchenko

SEA CHANGE
PO BOX 17832
BIRMINGHAM
B 13 3QB
UK

Fairtry III is one of the big fishing
trawlers, is one of the most common of
high production fishing. It is huge.
And there's a lot of them out there.
Remember that.

The humphead wrasse is a large, friendly
reef fish often referred to as the king of
the reef. Overfishing and the live fish
trade have contributed to a decline in its
population and it is currently endangered.

Humphead wrasses consume crustaceans,
molluscs and starfish. Without them coral
predators such as the crown of thorns
starfish are more abundant, threatening
the well being of large areas of coral reefs.

Help by supporting sustainable fishing
initiatives and oppose illegal trading so
our reefs can SEA change.

Vassiliki Tzomaka

*Then Algy looks a trifle glum,
"I'm going home," he tells his chum.*

SEA CHANGE
PO Box 17832
BIRMINGHAM
B13 3QB
UK

71   Vassiliki Tzomaka – UK/Greece

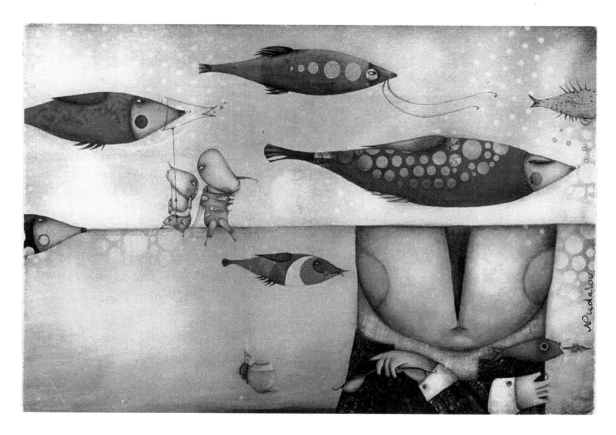

Natalie Pudalov – Israel   72

"The greatest danger to our planet,
is belief that someone else will save it."

Robert Swan

The whale swims underneath the city.
Deep down among the roots of steel and concrete,
Where pipes and cables wave like kelp.
Its low voice is held inside the groan of traffic.
Where neon splashes on the tarmac you will see a ripple,
And you'll see, in the small, salt pools of every cell,
The echo of its passing.

Nicola Davies – UK

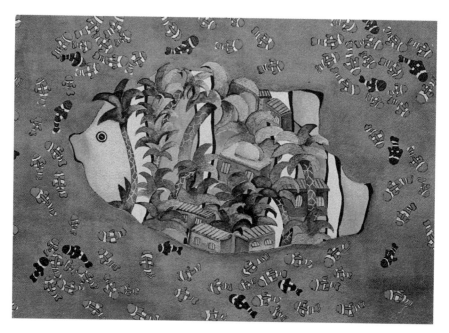

This is the map of Kish Island in Iran which is very similar to the shape of a fish. The surrounding clownfish are found in the Persian Gulf but are endangered due to climate change and over-fishing.

Adria Shokouhi Razi – Iran   76

TAKE ACTION FOR THE OCEAN

Please leave this place as you would like your children to find it.

79   Petr Horáček – UK/Czech Republic

Martina Walther –   Switzerland   80

Take good care to the seas and all
the little sparkling beauties in it!

oceans of love

PROTECT OUR OCEAN, PROTECT OUR FUTURE.

FROM:
EMILA YUSOF
KL

SEA CHANGE
PO BOX 17832
BIRMINGHAM
B13 3QB
UNITED KINGDOM

THE OCEAN GIRL & THE BARRAMUNDI (PENCIL + COLOUR PENCIL)

Protect our ocean,
Protect our future.

Emila Yusof – Malaysia

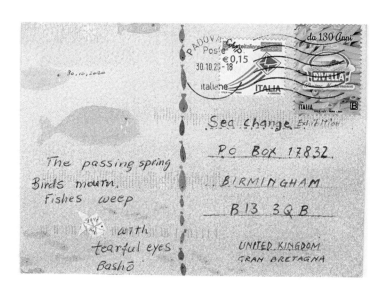

The passing spring
Birds mourn,
Fishes weep
With tearful eyes.

Matsuo Bashō

Andreina Parpajola – Italy

David Álvarez – Mexico   86

We need another and a
wiser and perhaps a more
mystical concept of animals.

Henry Beston

Protect life in our oceans!

89   Yuxing Li – Germany/China

Protect sea turtles,
healthy oceans need
Sea Turtles!

From
Illustration by Sara Tashnizi

210408D057 ///////////
3810 M4L

CANADA 27

To:
SEA CHANGE
PO BOX 17832
BIRMINGHAM
B13 3QB
UK

Protect sea turtles.
Healthy oceans need sea turtles.

91

Sara Tashnizi – Canada

Where are my friends?
Where is my home?
Be the change.

Be Human Design – Taiwan

Klaas Verplancke – Belgium   94

SAVE OUR SEAS!

(and the oceans and the fish
and the polar bears
and the mermaids....)

KEEP THEM CLEAN!

Darshika Varma – India

The flutter of a fin
can cause a wave.
Come together,
we've a world to save.

Chitra Soundar

Care for the sea!

99   Mies van Hout – Netherlands

Message in a Bottle:
Our seas are amazing,
full of life and wonder.
Our responsibility is to
care for the life they hold
and to keep them clean.

Tatyana Feeney,
Ireland
tatyanaks@hotmail.com

To: SEA ∞
      CHANGE

PO Box 17832
Birmingham
B13 3QB
UK

Our seas are amazing,
full of life and wonder.
Our responsibility is to
care for the life they hold
and to keep them clean.

Tatyana Feeney – Ireland/USA

It's a beautiful planet,
let's live TOGETHER!

Bengü Çimendag– Turkey

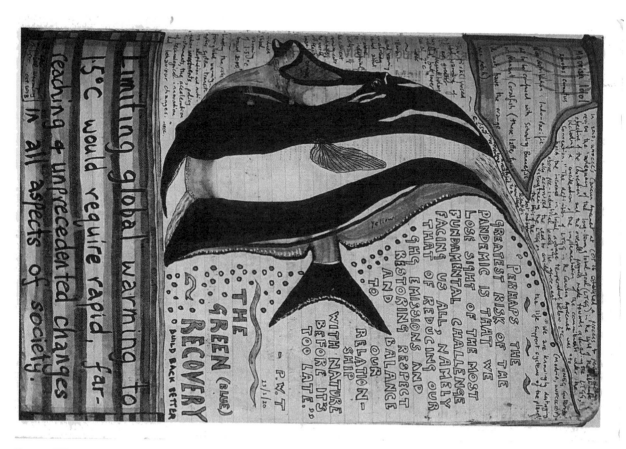

Limiting global warming to 1.5°C would require rapid, far-reaching 4 unprecedented changes in all aspects of society.

PERHAPS THE GREATEST RISK OF THE PANDEMIC IS THAT WE LOSE SIGHT OF THE MOST FUNDAMENTAL CHALLENGE FACING US ALL: NAMELY THAT OF REDUCING OUR GHG EMISSIONS AND RESTORING RESPECT AND BALANCE TO OUR RELATION-SHIP WITH NATURE BEFORE IT'S TOO LATE.

- P.W.T
13/3/20

THE GREEN (BLUE) RECOVERY

o o BUILD BACK BETTER

Peter Thomson – Fiji   104

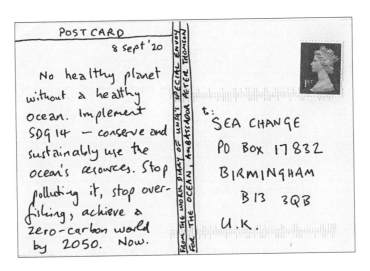

No healthy planet without a healthy ocean. Implement SDG 14 – conserve and sustainably use the ocean's resources. Stop polluting it, stop over-fishing, achieve a zero-carbon world by 2050.

NOW!

EDITOR

TOBIAS HICKEY is a founder, with Piet Grobler, of the International Centre for the Picture Book in Society, based at the University of Worcester's School of Arts, where he is a Senior Lecturer and Course Leader in Illustration.

CONTRIBUTORS

SENA AHADJI's motto is "Be the change!" An ardent advocate of triggering the creativity of young people to bring about progressive change in society, she lives in Accra.

MARTÍ ALCON was born in Olesa de Montserrat in Catalonia, and still lives there. A graduate of Escola de la Dona in Barcelona, she is illustrator of *Return al Sol*, by Josep Maria Francès (2018 edition).

DAVID ÁLVAREZ is a freelance author and illustrator, based in Mexico City. A graduate of the Design School of the National Institute of Fine Arts and Literature, his *Bandada* (text by Maria Julia Garrido), won the International Compostela Picture Book Prize (2012).

MIMI AZRIN is an artist and illustrator. Fine cooking and artistic needlework also figure in her repertoire of skills. She lives in Sungai Buloh, Selangor, Malaysia.

CATHERINE BARR is a leading writer of children's books with conservation themes. *Invisible Nature* (illustrated by Anne Wilson) won the Teach Primary non-fiction award in 2020. She lives in Herefordshire, on the English-Welsh border.

BARROUX was born in Paris but grew up in Morocco and has also lived in Canada and the USA. His most recent picture book, *I Love You, Blue* (2021) is a story of friendship between a lighthouse keeper and a whale. He lives in Montreuil, France.

BE HUMAN DESIGN is based in Kaohsiung City, Taiwan, and run by Hsiang-Ying Chen and Ying-Hsiu Chen. Much of their work is child-related. They were finalists in the Bologna Illustrators Exibition 2021, and winners in 2019.

KAROL BERNAL is a Catalan illustrator who enjoys experimenting with new techniques and registers. She studied illustration at the Escola de la Dona in Barcelona, and currently divides her time between Barcelona and Amposta (Tarragona).

RENATA BUENO is an artist and architect, with over 40 books published. She enjoys creating playful books for children, using a variety of techniques. Winner of Brazil's

prestigious Jabuti Prize for illustration in 2013, she currently lives in Portugal.

BENGÜ ÇIMENDAG describes himself as "a creative person, fond of earth, earthlings and universe." He is founder of Studio Mundus, an independent illustration shop in Istanbul.

ANDY ROBERT DAVIES is a lecturer in illustration at Worcester University and an illustrator of children's and adult books and magazines. He lives in Worcestershire.

NICOLA DAVIES has written many books for children, about nature and wildlife, as well as being an accomplished artist. *The Star Whale*, with illustrations by Petr Horáček, will be published by Otter-Barry Books in September 2023. She lives in Wales.

MARION DEUCHARS was born in Scotland and graduated with distinction from the Royal College of Art, London. She is author/illustrator of many books including the *'Let's Make Some Great Art'* activity books. She lives in North London.

MOHAMMAD BARRANGI FASHTAMI was born in Rasht, northern Iran, and now lives in England. He writes: "I am both an artist and an athlete. I have a disability in my left hand, though I believe it is by no means a stymying limitation … I love printmaking. I make them with my hand and using my leg."

TATYANA FEENEY grew up in North Carolina, USA, and now lives in County Meath, Ireland. She enjoys doing storytime sessions and art workshops. Her books include *Eva and the Perfect Rain* and *Little Owl's Orange Scarf*, which won the Rotherham Picture Book Award, 2014.

STEPHEN FOWLER specialises in rubber stamping and alternative print making. He grew up in Cornwall, graduated at Central St Martin's School of Art in London, and is a Lecturer in Illustration at the University of Worcester's School of Arts.

ALI GHORBANIMOGHADDAM, born in Teheran, is studying medicine in Munich, Germany. He has been illustrating children's books since 2013 and received the Golden Pinwheel Award of Excellence for Young Illustrators in Shanghai (2016).

PIET GROBLER is an award-winning South African illustrator and a graduate in Theology, Journalism and Visual Arts (Illustration). He is visiting professor in Illustration at the University of Worcester, UK and lives in Portugal.

YOSHIKO HADA was a winner in the Illustrators' Exhibition at the Bologna Children's Book Fair, 2021. She sees her work as "like alchemy that transforms monotonous everyday life into something wonderful." She is based in Tokyo.

PETR HORÁČEK was born in Prague and now lives in England. As an illustrator he has won many awards, including the Royal Society Young People's Book Prize in 2017, for *A First Book of Animals*. His picture book *The Last Tiger* is published in paperback in 2023.

MIES VAN HOUT majored in Graphic Design at the Arts Academy in Groningen and has been illustrating children's books for over 30 years. Her work has been published in more than twenty countries. She lives in the Netherlands.

VARVARA IASHCHENKO has a PhD in Biology and taught in the Centre for Biodiversity Dynamics at the Norwegian University of Science and Technology. Born in St Petersburg, Russia, she is now a professional illustrator, living in Oslo.

NADINE KAADAN is a children's book author and illustrator from Syria, now living in London. Nadine has been nominated for a Kate Greenaway Medal, was the 2019 winner

of the Arab British Centre Award for Culture and selected as one of The BBC 100 Women 2020's 'most influential and inspiring women'.

GUILHERME KARSTEN has 30-plus books, published in over 15 languages, to his credit. His international awards include a Golden Plaque at the Bratislava BIB (2019), and a Golden Pinwheel Grand Award (Shanghai, 2019). He lives in Blumenau, southern Brazil.

YUXING LI lives in Hamburg, Germany. She enjoys working on art techniques with children and is co-founder of Kinderkunst-workshops. Among her awards are a Special Mention in the Hiii Illustration Awards 2021, and the Illustrarte Grand Prix in 2018.

MARÍA LEÓN is a Spanish nature artist who describes herself as "an enthusiastic biologist who likes to observe nature and paint around that." Born in A Coruña, she lives in Tarifa, Andalucia.

JULIE McALLISTER's art career began with the Bernina Encouragement Award in 2012 and since then her quilt designs have won prizes and been widely exhibited in international shows. She was born and still lives in Perth, Western Australia.

HEDIE MEISCHKE grew up in The Hague, where she studied at the Royal Academy of Art. Hedie received an Honourable Mention in the 2020 Picture This! competition for *Rinaldo's Voice*. She lives in Overijssel, Netherlands.

ROGER MELLO was born in Brasilia and now lives in Rio de Janeiro. Among his many distinctions, he was winner of the Hans Christian Andersen Illustration Award in 2014. Roger works extensively with IBBY for international understanding through children's books.

SARAH MILLIN studied textile design at Chelsea College of Art, London, and then worked as a textile designer in Kenya. As a freelance illustrator she has done much work for organisations concerned with children, including World Fish Migration Day. She lives in Worcestershire, England.

JACKIE MORRIS is a writer and artist with a profound sensitivity to the natural world, famed for her illustrations for *The Lost Words* (text by Robert Macfarlane), chosen by British booksellers as the most beautiful book of 2017. She lives in Wales.

VIIVE NOOR is founder of the Tallinn Illustration Triennial, and a curator of the Estonian Children's Literature Centre. A graduate of the Estonian State Art Institute, her awards include the IBBY Honour List (2006) and the Golden Pen at the Belgrade International Biennale of Illustrations (2013).

ARÉVIK D'OR's first book, *Giro* (2017), was selected for the prestigious 'White Ravens' list of best children's books in 2018. Based in Belgium, she is a freelance illustrator, animator, animation film director and workshop coach.

ANDREINA PARPAJOLA is an author and illustrator based in Padua, Italy. She combines a special interest in Japanese art and culture with a 30-year career in illustration, most recently *The Book of Tea* (2020).

ANDREJA PEKLAR is a leading Slovene illustrator, living in Ljubljana, Slovenia. A graduate of the Ljubljana Academy of Fine Arts, she featured on the IBBY Honour List in 2018, and has received an Award of Excellence at the Bologna Children's Book Fair, 2018.

CRISTINA PIEROPAN has illustrated over 25 picture books and her work has been featured at Itabashi Art Museum, Tokyo; BIB Biennial, Bratislava; Nami Concours, Korea; and many other places. She lives in Castelfranco Veneto, Italy.

NATALIE PUDALOV was born in Russia and moved with her parents to Israel. A graduate of the Bezalel Academy of Art & Design in Jerusalem and the Stuttgart Academy of Art & Design, she says of her work, "That's my world, the world of creatures, animals and nature."

JANE RAY has worked as illustrator with many celebrated authors, and was nominated for the Hans Christian Andersen Award by IBBY UK in 2018. A winner of the Smarties Award (1992) she has been shortlisted six times for the Kate Greenaway Award.

ADRIA SHOKOUHI RAZI is an Iranian illustrator. She writes, "I love spending my time illustrating and crafting and have a deep interest in illustrating kids' books." She lives in Teheran.

KATHLEEN RICHENS' delicate watercolour illustrations are full of intriguing detail. With a degree in Geography, she has an informed understanding of the plight of the ocean. She lives in Canterbury region, New Zealand.

AXEL SCHEFFLER has illustrated some of the world's best-loved children's books, incuding the Gruffalo series (with Julia Donaldson). Born in Hamburg, Germany, he now lives in London.

CHITRA SOUNDAR is an internationally published author of over 50 books for children, many of them inspired by Indian folktales. She lives in London.

MAYA STANIC grew up in Bosnia-Herzegovina and has a master's degree in product design from Sarajevo Academy of Art and Design. She is now based in London, and her fine work in stained glass can be seen in many locations.

SARA TASHNIZI was born in Iran and is a freelance illustrator based in Toronto, Canada. She graduated in Visual Art at Soore University, Teheran, and has also studied in the School of Arts, Media, Performance and Design at York University, Toronto.

PETER THOMSON is the UN Secretary-General's Special Envoy for the Ocean. His role is to lead UN advocacy and outreach to galvanise political momentum, mobilise action, and raise ambition for the implementation of the UN's Sustainable Development Goal 14.

VASSILIKI TZOMAKA has a PhD in children's book illustration from the Cambridge School of Art, as well as degrees in Chemistry and Environmental Studies. She lectures at the University of Suffolk, England.

DARSHIKA VARMA was born and grew up in Mumbai, India. She studied for a BFA at Rachana Sansad in Mumbai, and specialises in books for younger children, both fiction and non-fiction.

NELLEKE VERHOEFF began as a performer but found her true vocation in art and illustration. Her book *Concerto* was a finalist in the 2018 Silent Book Competition. She lives in Rotterdam, Netherlands.

KLAAS VERPLANCKE is an internationally acclaimed illustrator, author, art director and animator. He has received 17 nominations for the Astrid Lindgren Memorial Award, a Special Mention in the Bologna Ragazzi Awards, and has books in the IBBY Honours and 'White Ravens' lists.

SABINE WALDMANN-BRUN combines two careers, teaching painting, glass design and illustration at the Stuttgart Academy of Creative Arts; and medical history and ethics at Tübingen University.

MARTINA WALTHER is a graduate of the Hochschule Design & Kunst, Lucerne. Since 2014 she has participated in many international exhibitions and was a finalist in the Golden Pinwheel Award (China, 2019). She lives in Konolfingen, Switzerland.

ANNE WILSON has an MA in Illustration from Central St Martin's College of Art, London. *Invisible Nature*, with text by Catherine Barr, won the Teach Primary non-fiction award in 2020. She lives in Surrey, England.

KEN WILSON-MAX, author, illustrator and publisher, was born in Zimbabwe and now lives in London. *Astro Girl* won the UK STEAM Award for early years picture books in 2020.

EMILA YUSOF was born in Raub, Pahang, Malaysia. Self-taught, she has been a picture book illustrator since 2007. Her awards include the Little Hakka Merit Award 2017 (China) for *Grandma's Flowering Tea*. She lives in Kuala Lumpur.

YUVAL ZOMMER is a graduate of the Royal College of Art, London, and renowned for children's books that put the living world at the heart of storytelling. *His Big Book of Beasts* won the English Association's 4-11 Best Book Award in 2018.